Raintree is an imprint of Capstone Global Library Limited, a company incorporated in England and Wales having its registered office at 7 Pilgrim Street, London, EC4V 6LB – Registered company number: 6695582

www.raintree.co.uk
myorders@raintree.co.uk

Edited by James Benefield and Eliza Leahy
Designed by Bob Lentz
Original illustrations © Hanna-Barbera 2015
Illustrated by Scott Jeralds
Production by Gene Bentdahl
Printed in China by Nordica
0914/CA21401580

ISBN 978-1-4062-9241-1 (paperback)
18 17 16 15 14
10 9 8 7 6 5 4 3 2 1

British Library Cataloguing in Publication Data
A full catalogue record for this book is available from the British Library.

Acknowledgements
Every effort has been made to contact copyright holders of material reproduced in this book. Any omissions will be rectified in subsequent printings if notice is given to the publisher.

All the Internet addresses (URLs) given in this book were valid at the time of going to press. However, due to the dynamic nature of the Internet, some addresses may have changed, or sites may have changed or ceased to exist since publication. While the author and publisher regret any inconvenience this may cause readers, no responsibility for any such changes can be accepted by either the author or the publisher.

Set List:

What's the best way to help a starving zombie?
Give him a hand!

When do zombies go to sleep?
Only when they're dead tired.

What do zombies like to eat when they go out to a restaurant?

The waiters!

Where's the safest place in your house to hide from zombies?
The *living* room, of course.

What does Godzilla call skateboarders?

Meals on wheels!

Why is Godzilla so good at sneaking up on people?
He's a crept-ile.

What did Godzilla say when he saw a train full of passengers?
"Chew-chew!"

What's the best way to call Godzilla?
Long distance!

Why did Godzilla eat all the furniture in the hotel room?
He had a suite tooth!

Did you hear that Godzilla was sick?
Yeah, it's all over town!

What do you call Godzilla
in a phone box?

Stuck!

How does Dracula like his coffee?
De-coffin-ated!

When did Dracula realize that sunlight could destroy him?

When it finally *dawned* on him!

What kind of dog does Dracula have?
A bloodhound!

Why won't anyone kiss Dracula?
He has *bat* breath!

Why was the vampire studying all night long?
She was getting ready for her blood test!

What do you say to a vampire who wants to go on a date?
"Fangs, but no fangs!"

Why don't vampires have many friends?

They're such pains in the neck!

What's a vampire's favourite fruit?
Neck-tarines.

Why did the zombie lose the card game?
He had a rotten hand!

What do you call a zombie
door-to-door salesman?

A dead-ringer!

What happened when the zombie was late for the dinner party?
They gave him the cold shoulder.

What do you call a teenage zombie with no legs?
Grounded.

What did the zombie do when she lost her hand?
She went to the *secondhand* shop!

What did the little zombie make of his new friends at school?
A pie!

What did the zombie eat after the dentist pulled out all his teeth?
The dentist!

Don't make a vampire angry. **They have very *bat* tempers!**

What does Dracula take when he has a cold?
Coffin medicine!

What do goblins like to put on their toast?
Scream cheese!

That vampire certainly is popular.

Yeah, she has a big fang club.

How did the vampire cure his sore throat?
He spent all day gargoyling!

What do little vampires eat for lunch?
Alpha-bat soup.

Where does Dracula keep his money?
In a blood bank.

Why don't vampires ever race each other?
They're always neck and neck!

Did you know there's a vampire duck?
Of course. It's Count Quackula!

Why did the vampire fail her art exam?
She could only *draw blood!*

I heard the new restaurant has a vampire for a chef.
Yes, he's Count Spatula!

What do you get if you cross the Mystery Machine with a bloodsucker?

A van-pire!

What do you call a ghost's mum and dad?
Trans-parents!

What do you call a ghost that haunts chickens?
A poultry-geist!

What keeps a ghost cool in the summer?
A scare conditioner.

What did the ghost wear to the dinner party?
A boo tie!

In what position do ghosts sleep?
Horror-zontal!

Where do ghosts go for treats?
The I-scream parlour!

Where do phantoms post their letters?
A ghost office!

What do you say to a ghost when you meet one?
"How do you boo?"

What do baby ghosts wear on their feet?
Boo-ties!

Did you hear that
Dr Frankenstein combined a
cocker spaniel, a poodle
and a ghost?

Yep, he ended up with a cocker-poodle-boo!

What do teenage ghosts wear?
Boo jeans.

What's the first thing ghosts do when they get
into a car?
Put on their sheet belts!

Why are ghosts so bad at telling lies?
**You can always see right through
them.**

How do ghosts like their eggs cooked?
Terror-fried!

Why do ghosts take the lift?
It raises their spirits!

What happened to
the mad scientist who
crossed a pig with a
grizzly bear?

**He got a
teddy boar!**

What happened to
the mad scientist who
crossed a UFO with a
wizard?

**He got a
flying sorcerer!**

What happened to
the mad scientist who
crossed a slab of cheese
with Frankenstein?

**He got a really
scary Muenster!**

What happened to
the mad scientist who
crossed a snake with
some building blocks?
**He got a
boa constructor!**

What happened to
the mad scientist who
crossed a turtle with a
porcupine?
**He got a
slowpoke.**

What happened to
the mad scientist who
crossed a toad with a
distant galaxy?
**He got star
warts!**

What happened to the mad scientist who crossed a bear cub with a skunk?

He got Winnie the Phew!

What happened to the mad scientist who crossed a newborn snake with a trampoline?

He got a bouncing baby boa!

What happened to the mad scientist who crossed an alligator with a rabbit?

He had to get a new rabbit!

Why didn't the skeleton go to the school disco?
He had no *body* to go with!

Why was the skeleton so afraid of heights?
She just didn't have the guts!

Why did the skeleton keep his head in the freezer?
I suppose he was a numbskull!

Why didn't the skeleton eat the canteen food?
He didn't have the stomach for it.

Where do skeletons go on holiday?
The Dead Sea!

Where can you always find a cemetery?
In the dead centre of town.

What did the film director say when she had finished
her mummy film?
"That's a wrap!"

The doctor told the mummy he had the heart of a
much younger man.
**Yes, and the doctor told him he had
to give it back, too!**

Did you know that skeletons love riding motorbikes?
Yep, they're _bone_ to be wild!

What do skeletons order when they go to a restaurant?
Spare ribs!

What did the skeleton dad say
to his son when he stayed in
bed all day?

"Lazy bones!"

Why doesn't the mummy have any friends?
She's too *wrapped up* in herself!

What did the ghost say to his girlfriend?
"I really dig you!"

What does a skeleton say before every meal?
"Bone appétit!"

Who won the skeleton beauty contest?
No body!

Cemeteries are having difficulty finding room for all their guests.

Yes, it's a *grave* problem!

Why did Frankenstein go to the psychiatrist?
He thought he had a screw loose!

Why did Frankenstein go to the restaurant
with a raisin?
He couldn't find a date!

What's Frankenstein's favourite pudding?
I scream!!!

Do you know where Frankenstein lives?
Yes, at a dead end.

I heard that Dr Frankenstein is really funny.
Yeah, he always keeps you in *stitches*!

Why is Dr Frankenstein so popular?

He's very good at making friends.

How does Frankenstein eat his lunch?
He bolts it down!

What does it say on Frankenstein's gravestone?
"Rest in Pieces."

How did Frankenstein get rid of his headache?
**He put his head through a window
and the pane just disappeared!**

What did Frankenstein say to the screwdriver?
"Daddy!"

What do you call witches who live in the same room?
Broom-mates!

What do you call a nervous witch?
A twitch!

Watch out! We're being chased by twin sorceresses!
I know! I can't tell witch is witch!

Why was the witch late for the party?
Her broom overswept.

How does a wizard tell the time?
With a witch-watch!

What do you get when you cross a witch's cat with a lemon?
A sourpuss.

Did you know that witches fall from the sky?
Yeah, and the angry ones fly off the handle!

What happened to the wizard who was badly behaved at school?

He got ex-*spelled!*

What kind of sorceress is always helpful in the dark?

A lights-witch!

What happened when the giant brick monster escaped from prison?

They set up a road block!

What happened when the Human Fly
escaped from prison?
They brought in a SWAT team!

What happened when the cyclops escaped
from prison?
The police had to keep an eye open!

What happened when the evil
hairdresser escaped from prison?

Police had to comb
the area!

What happened when the mutant corn monster escaped from prison?

They called out the cobs!

What happened when a gang of monsters escaped through the sewers?

The police said it was a grime wave!

Bit eight:
Werewolves, aliens and other creepy crawlies!

Why didn't the monster ever go out with his friends after school?

He wasn't allowed to play with his food!

How many parents does a werewolf have?

Five. One ma and four paws.

What does a techie pirate wear?

An iPatch.

What should you do if you're attacked by a gang of clowns?

Go for the juggler!

What monster eats the fastest?
A goblin!

What planet did the evil aliens crash land on?
Splaturn!

What technique do aliens use for fighting?
Martian arts!

Why do dragons sleep during the day?
So they can fight knights!

Who's the centre of attention at a
monster disco?
The boogie man!

Which hand should you use to stroke
King Kong?

Someone else's!

How can you tell if there's a monster under your bed?
Your nose touches the ceiling!

What did Godzilla say after he caused
an earthquake?
"Sorry, my fault!"

What do sea monsters like to eat?
Fish and ships!

Why did the headless horseman go to university?
He wanted to get *a head* in life!

Why did the monster's gran knit him a new sock?
She heard that he'd grown another foot!

How do you mend a broken jack-o'-lantern?
With a pumpkin patch!

Why did King Kong climb the Empire State Building?

He was too big to use the stairs!

What do you call a one-eyed monster on a motorbike?
A cycle-ops!

How can I contact the Loch Ness monster?

Drop it a line!

What monster is grey, has a long trunk and wears a mask?

The Elephantom of the Opera!

Why is a cemetery a great place to write a book?
It's full of plots!

Where does the yeti keep its money?
In a snow bank.

What would you say if you saw two cyclopes in a dark alley?
"Eye, eye!"

What happened to the man who didn't pay his exorcist?

He got re-possessed!

Did you hear about the monster who was a Star Trek fan?
He had one right ear, one left ear, and one final front-ear!

Why are ghost children so happy at the end of the week?
It's Fright Day!

What happened when the vampire bit into the cake?
She got frostingbite!

What do ghosts use to wash their hair?
Sham-boo.

Why did the scarecrow win the Nobel Prize?
He was outstanding in his field!

Who is the scariest singer on the planet?
The Grim Rapper.

What's a monster's favourite play?

Romeo and Ghouliet!

Why did it take so long for Godzilla to gobble up
Big Ben?
It was time-consuming!

What do you call a hairy monster flying a helicopter?
A whirr-wolf!

Why did the zombie get a massage?
She was a little stiff!

SHAGGY: Poor Scooby! The police put him in prison
after he ran away from the slime monster.
FRED: Why?
SHAGGY: **He was arrested for leaving
the scene of the grime!**

How to Tell Jokes!

1. KNOW the joke
Make sure you remember the whole joke before you tell it. This sounds obvious, but most of us know someone who says, "Oh, this is so funny..." Then, when they tell the joke, they can't remember the end. And that's the whole point of a joke – its punchline.

2. SPEAK CLEARLY
Don't mumble: don't speak too quickly or too slowly. Just speak like you normally do. You don't have to use a different voice or accent or sound like someone else. (UNLESS that's part of the joke!)

3. LOOK at your audience
Good eye contact with your listeners will grab their attention.

4. DON'T WORRY about gestures or how to stand or sit
when you tell your joke. Remember, telling a joke is basically talking.

5. DON'T LAUGH at your own joke
Yeah, yeah, I know some comedians crack up while they're acting in a sketch or telling a story, but the best rule to follow is not to laugh. If you start to laugh, you might lose the rhythm of your joke or stop yourself from telling the joke clearly. Let your audience laugh. That's their job. Your job is to be the funny one.

6. THE PUNCHLINE is the most important part of the joke
It's the climax, the reward, the main event. A good joke can sound even better if you pause for just a second or two before you deliver the punchline. That tiny pause will make your audience mentally sit up and hold their breath, eager to hear what's coming next.

7. The SETUP is the second most important part of a joke

That's basically everything you say before you get to the punchline. And that's why you need to be as clear as you can (see 2 above) so that when you finally reach the punchline, it makes sense!

8. YOU CAN GET FUNNIER

It's easy. Watch other comedians. Listen to other people tell a joke or story. Go and see a good comedy show or film. You can pick up some skills simply by seeing how others get their comedy across. You will absorb it! And soon it will come naturally.

9. Last, but not least, telling a joke is all about TIMING

That means not only getting the biggest impact for your joke, waiting for the right time, giving that extra pause before the punchline — but it also means knowing when NOT to tell a joke. When you're among friends, you can tell when they'd like to hear something funny. But in an unfamiliar setting, get a "sense of the room" first. Are people having a good time? Or is it a more serious event? A joke has the most funny power when it's told in the right setting.

Michael Dahl

How is **Michael Dahl** like a vampire at the library?
They both want a good book they can sink their teeth into!

When Dahl is not reading good books, he's writing them. He has penned more than two hundred books for young readers. He is the author of *The Everything Kids' Joke Book*, *Laff-O-Tronic Joke Books*, the scintillating *Duck Goes Potty* and two humorous mystery series: Finnegan Zwake and Hocus Pocus Hotel. He has toured the United States with an improv troupe and began his auspicious comic career at primary school when his stand-up routine made his music teacher laugh so hard she fell off her chair. She is not available for comment.

Scott Jeralds

Why did the Abominable Snowman ask **Scott Jeralds** to draw his portrait?
Because he's a cool artist!

Jeralds has worked in animation for companies including Marvel Studios, Hanna-Barbera Studios, M.G.M. Animation, Warner Bros. and Porchlight Entertainment. Scott has worked on TV series such as *The Flintstones*, *Yogi Bear*, *Scooby-Doo*, *The Jetsons*, *Krypto the Superdog*, *Tom and Jerry*, *The Pink Panther*, *Superman*, *Secret Saturdays* and he directed the cartoon series *Freakazoid*, for which he won an Emmy Award. In addition, Scott has designed cartoon-related merchandise, licensing art, and artwork for several comic and children's book publications.

Joke Dictionary!

bit section of a comedy routine

comedian entertainer who makes people laugh

headliner last comedian to perform in a show

improvisation performance that hasn't been planned: "improv" for short

lineup list of people who are going to perform in a show

one-liner short joke or funny remark

open mike event at which anyone can use the microphone to perform for the audience

punchline words at the end of a joke that make it funny or surprising

shtick repetitive, comic performance or routine

segue sentence or phrase that leads from one joke or routine to another

stand-up type of comedy performed while standing alone on stage

timing use of rhythm and tempo to make a joke funnier

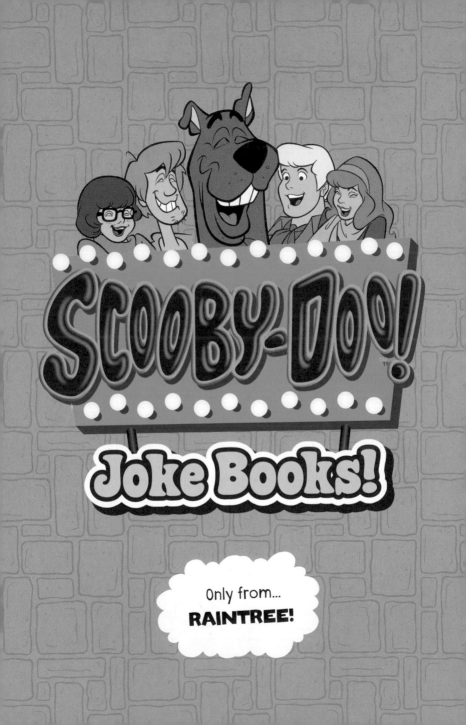

SCOOBY-DOO!

Joke Books!

Only from...
RAINTREE!

The fun
doesn't
stop here!

Discover more at...
raintree.co.uk